# SIAMESE FIGHTING FISH

## A TRUE BOOK

by

### Elaine Landau

**Children's Press®**
A Division of Grolier Publishing

New York  London  Hong Kong  Sydney
Danbury, Connecticut

*Reading Consultant*
**Linda Cornwell**
*Learning Resource Consultant*
*Indiana Department*
*of Education*

A Siamese
fighting fish

**Visit Children's Press® on the
Internet at:
http://publishing.grolier.com**

Library of Congress Cataloging-in-Publication Data

Landau, Elaine.
    Siamese fighting fish / by Elaine Landau.
        p.    cm. — (A true book)
    Includes bibliographical references and index.
    Summary: Introduces the physical characteristics, life cycle, and fierce
behavior of the Siamese fighting fish, also identifying differences between
those in the wild and those bred for sale in pet shops.
    ISBN: 0-516-20678-8 (lib. bdg.)   0-516-26504-0 (pbk.)
    1. Siamese fighting fish—Juvenile literature.   [1. Siamese fighting fish.]
I. Title.   II. Series.
SF458.B4L35   1999
639.3`77—dc21                                              98-16119
                                                              CIP
                                                               AC

**GROLIER**
PUBLISHING

# Contents

Siamese fighting
fish can be found
in many colors.

# A Beautiful Fish

What kind of fish might be described as beautiful but fierce? Hint: It is sold in pet shops everywhere. If you think it's a Siamese fighting fish, you are right!

Siamese fighting fish are creatures of many colors. They are found in shades of bright red, blue, and violet. There are also Siamese fighting fish that are green, yellow, or black. Some are even multicolored. Others are pale pink. Once in a while, you may even find a completely white one. A fish without any natural color is called an albino (al-BYE-noh).

Male Siamese fighting fish are a little less than 3 inches (8 centimeters) long. They have graceful, flowing fins.

In this photograph, you can easily see the difference between male (top) and female (bottom) Siamese fighting fish.

The females measure just over 2 inches (5 cm). Their fins are shorter than the males' fins.

#  Bettas

A multicolored Betta

Many home aquariums contain Bettas.

The scientific name for Siamese fighting fish is Betta splendens (BAY-tuh SPLEN-denz). Many people simply call them "Bettas."

In their natural surroundings, Siamese fighting fish look a lot different from the kinds sold in pet stores.

The Siamese fighting fish you see in pet shops are bred, or specially raised, for their beauty. Those you may see in the wild look so different that you might not even think the two fish were related. In their natural habitat, Siamese fighting fish have short fins. They are usually dull brown or grey-green in color. Some have dark stripes across their bodies.

In the wild, Siamese fighting fish are found in Thailand (TYE-land). Thailand is a country in Southeast Asia. Thailand was once known as Siam. That is why these fish are called Siamese fighting fish. In Thailand, they live in weed-filled watery ditches near rice paddies.

NEPAL · BHUTAN · CHINA · ASIA · INDIA · BANGLADESH · MYANMAR · LAOS · TAIWAN · SOUTH CHINA SEA · BAY OF BENGAL · THAILAND · VIETNAM · PHILIPPINES · CAMBODIA · SRI LANKA · BRUNEI · INDIAN OCEAN · Equator · MALAYSIA · INDONESIA

Area of Detail

0     400 miles

0     600 kilometers

Siamese fighting fish originally come from watery areas in Thailand (above). Rice paddies (right) are water-covered fields where rice grows.

Life in these small, crowded water holes can be difficult. Siamese fighting fish display some of the aggressive, or fierce, behavior that helps them survive.

Although Siamese fighting fish that are bred in aquariums look quite different from those in the wild, they are just as aggressive. (Aquariums are glass tanks in which you can keep fish.)

# An Unusual Trait

A trait is a quality, or characteristic, that makes a person or animal different from another. Siamese fighting fish have an interesting trait that makes them different from other fish.

Like other fish, Siamese fighting fish breathe through

Siamese fighting fish (right) have a unique characteristic that sets them apart from other fish. Fish (below) breathe oxygen from the water through organs called gills.

gills. (The gills are the organs that a fish uses to breathe oxygen from the water.) But Siamese fighting fish do not get all of their oxygen from the water. Instead, they have an extra breathing organ. This organ is known as a labyrinth (LA-buh-rinth). The labyrinth allows them to take oxygen directly from the air at the water's surface.

This added breathing organ also helps Siamese fighting

A Siamese fighting fish approaches the water's surface to breathe.

fish to survive in their natural environment. The small water holes they live in do not contain much oxygen. They are also very crowded. But since Siamese fighting fish can also take oxygen from the air, they can survive in less water than other fish.

Siamese fighting fish can be kept in small bowls or containers because they have a labyrinth.

# Fierce Fighters

If you are wondering if Siamese fighting fish really fight, the answer is yes. If you put two male Siamese fighting fish in a small space together, they will usually attack each other. They will keep fighting until one of them is either badly injured or

In this pet store (left), Siamese fighting fish are kept in their own separate tanks to prevent fighting. Many pet stores sell tank dividers (right) in different sizes. These dividers can be used to separate Siamese fighting fish.

dead. Male Siamese fighting fish usually fight over territory and females.

If many Siamese fighting fish live in one small space, reproducing is difficult.

This behavior may be a result of their living conditions in the wild. The areas that Siamese fighting fish live in are so crowded with other fish that some males can not reproduce. The weaker fish are injured or killed in the fights. The winning males take over the territory. They are then able to reproduce.

The same kind of brutal combat takes place in fish tanks. First, the males spread

A Siamese fighting fish spreads its fins in preparation for a fight.

their fins. This is a sign of aggression. They circle each other in the water. Then one comes forward to bite the other. Siamese fighting fish usually strike near the fins, the gills, or the eyes and head.

A bite from a Siamese fighting fish can do a lot of damage. This is because the teeth on this fish's lower jaw curve inward. They form sharp hooks. This is useful for trapping prey. It is a powerful weapon in fights as

Siamese fighting fish are equipped with powerful jaws for combat.

well. The jaws of the Siamese fighting fish are extremely powerful for such a small creature.

In Thailand, Siamese fighting fish were often set against one another for sport. The owners of these fish would put two different-colored males together in a small tank. People who were watching placed bets (money) on which fish would win. Quite a lot of money was spent in these contests. A fish known as an especially fierce fighter drew large crowds.

Surprisingly, a male Siamese fighting fish will not attack other species, or kinds, of male fish that are placed in the same tank. It can also be a

Under certain conditions, Siamese fighting fish can share a tank.

safe tank mate for male Siamese fighting fish that it has been raised with. It is a good tank mate for female Siamese fighting fish as well.

However, a female Siamese fighting fish sometimes will attack another female. It will nip at the other fish's fins or gills. But females do not usually fight to the death as males do.

Siamese fighting fish are actually slow swimmers. They

Small, newly hatched shrimp are called brine shrimp. They are good food for slow-swimming Siamese fighting fish.

eat prey that is easy to catch. In their natural environment, they feed mainly on water insects and small shrimp or crabs. They do not hunt smaller fish for food.

# Having Young

The eggs of most fish are fertilized outside of the female's body. However, Siamese fighting fish reproduce in a unique, or unusual, way. The process begins when the male fish builds a nest of bubbles. He makes the bubbles by blowing air through his mouth. These

Mucus is a substance that Siamese fighting fish produce to hold their bubble nest together.

bubbles are coated with a sticky substance. This substance is called mucus (MYOO-kuhss). Mucus comes from glands inside the fish's mouth.

A male Siamese fighting fish builds its bubble nest (above). These Siamese fighting fish are mating beneath the bubble nest (right).

It makes the bubbles hold together for a long time.

In a fish tank, the male builds its bubble nest near the water's surface. A female that is ready to mate then swims beneath the nest. The male fish meets her there. He wraps his body around her so that their vents, or openings, are close together. The female releases eggs that are ready for fertilization. The male releases sperm to fertilize these eggs.

The male Siamese fighting fish gathers the eggs for the bubble nest.

Afterward, the female sinks down in the tank to rest. The male quickly gathers up the fertilized eggs in its mouth. He then spits them into the bubble nest. The male and female repeat this process until the female has released all of her eggs.

From then on, the male takes care of the eggs. He drives the female away. If she does not leave the area, the

A male chasing the female away from the eggs.

male may attack her. (People who breed Siamese fighting fish often put the female into a different tank after mating.)

The male remains beneath the nest guarding the eggs. If an egg falls from the nest, he swims after it and brings it back. He also repairs the nest when it is necessary. He does this by replacing broken bubbles. After about forty hours, the eggs are hatched. The small fish swim off on their

If any of the fertilized eggs fall out of the bubble nest, the male replaces them (left). This is a young Siamese fighting fish (below).

own within three to four days. The male's work is done. He leaves the nest area for good.

# Fighting Fish As Pets

One or more Siamese fighting fish add a lot of color and interest to aquariums. Some people like these fish because they can be kept in smaller tanks than most fish.

When you buy a Siamese fighting fish—or any fish—ask a salesperson at the pet store

Colorful aquarium (top) setups can be complemented by colorful fish. A salesperson (left) can answer your questions and help you with your purchase.

This fish tank contains most of the equipment needed to begin an aquarium.

or aquarium shop to help you.
If you do not already have an
aquarium, find out what you
need to start one. The salesperson will be able to help you

set up a beginner's aquarium. You will also need instructions on how to feed and care for your fish. And keep the amount of money you have with you in mind as you shop. Home aquariums vary a great deal in cost.

When you choose Siamese fighting fish for your tank, try to learn how old the fish are. These fish live only about two years, so pick one that is just a few months old. A fish

Look carefully at all of the Siamese fighting fish before you choose one to take home.

that seems active in the tank and is interested in its environment is usually a good choice. Also, look for a fish with long, full fins that are not damaged or tattered. But do not buy a fighting fish with perfect fins if its body looks thin. This can be a sign of illness.

This is an example of a healthy Siamese fighting fish.

A Siamese fighting fish can be an excellent addition to a home aquarium.

Siamese fighting fish can be a great source of enjoyment. Kept under the proper conditions, these fish do not have to fight. Instead, they can bring much pleasure through their special beauty and grace.

# Keeping Siamese Fighting Fish

**H**ere are a few tips to help you keep healthy Siamese fighting fish:

• Siamese fighting fish can be kept in a container as small as a mayonnaise jar, or as large as several gallons.

• The water temperature should be 68 to 84 degrees Fahrenheit (20 to 29 degrees Celsius).

• Siamese fighting fish should be fed twice a day.

• The aquarium should not be placed in direct sunlight.

# To Find Out More

Here are some additional resources to help you learn more about fish and aquariums:

 **Books**

Aliki. **My Visit to the Aquarium.** HarperCollins, 1993.

Armstrong, Pam. **Young Explorer's Guide to Undersea Life.** Monterey Bay Aquarium Press, 1996.

Aronsky, Jim. **Crinkleroot's 25 Fish Every Child Should Know.** Bradbury Press, 1993.

Snedden, Robert. **What Is a Fish?** Sierra Club Books For Children, 1993.

## Organizations and Online Sites

### All About Bettas

*www.geocities.com/ RainForest/5411*

This site includes photographs, information on keeping and breeding Siamese fighting fish, and a guestbook you can sign.

### Betta Barracks

*www.aristotle.net/~vampyre/ index.html*

Everything you need to know about caring for Siamese fighting fish, including FAQ and links to other related sites.

### Betta Information

*www.aquariacentral.com/ fishinfo/fresh/betta.htm*

Here you'll find photographs, articles, and information about different species of Bettas. There's also a link to a site that details how to set up your own Betta aquarium.

### FINS

*http://www.actwin.com/fish*

FINS is the Fish Information Service—an archive of information about aquariums, including sites specific to angelfish.

### Fish and Wildlife Reference Service

5430 Grosvenor Lane
Suite 110
Bethesda, MD 20814

# Important Words

*combat*  a fight or struggle

*fertilize*  to make able to produce young

*habitat*  natural setting in which an animal lives

*paddies*  wet fields where rice is grown

*prey*  an animal that is hunted for food

*reproduce*  to create offspring or have young

*territory*  the area or region where an animal lives

# Index

# Meet the Author

Elaine Landau has a Bachelor of Arts degree in English and Journalism from New York University and a Masters degree in Library and Information Science from Pratt Institute. She has worked as a newspaper reporter, children's book editor, and a youth services librarian, but especially enjoys writing for young people.

Ms. Landau has written more than one hundred nonfiction books on various topics. She lives in Miami, Florida, with her husband Norman and son, Michael.